AUDIO ACCESS INCLUDED
Recorded Piano Accompaniments Online

PLAYBACK+
Speed • Pitch • Balance • Loop

SINGER'S JAZZ ANTHOLOGY | HIGH VOICE

classic standards

by Brent Edstrom

T0071269

To access audio visit:
www.halleonard.com/mylibrary
Enter Code
8245-2626-8630-7134

ISBN 978-1-5400-4192-0

HAL•LEONARD®

Visit Hal Leonard Online at
www.halleonard.com

Contact us:
Hal Leonard
7777 West Bluemound Road
Milwaukee, WI 53213
Email: info@halleonard.com

In Europe, contact:
Hal Leonard Europe Limited
42 Wigmore Street
Marylebone, London, W1U 2RN
Email: info@halleonardeurope.com

In Australia, contact:
Hal Leonard Australia Pty. Ltd.
4 Lentara Court
Cheltenham, Victoria, 3192 Australia
Email: info@halleonard.com.au

ARRANGER'S NOTE

The vocalist's part in the *Singer's Jazz Anthology* matches the original sheet music but is *not* intended to be sung verbatim. Instead, melodic embellishments and alterations of rhythm and phrasing should be incorporated to both personalize a performance and conform to the accompaniments. In some cases, the form has been expanded to include "tags" and other endings not found in the original sheet music. In these instances, the term *ad lib.* indicates new melodic material appended to the original form.

Although the concept of personalizing rhythms and embellishing melodies might seem awkward to singers who specialize in classical music, there is a long tradition of melodic variation within the context of performance dating back to the Baroque. Not only do jazz singers personalize a given melody to fit the style of an accompaniment, they also develop a distinctive sound that helps *further* personalize their performances. Undoubtedly, the best strategy for learning how to stylize a jazz melody is to listen to recordings from the vocal jazz canon, including artists such as Nat King Cole, Ella Fitzgerald, Billie Holiday, Frank Sinatra, Sarah Vaughan, Nancy Wilson, and others.

The accompaniments in the *Singer's Jazz Anthology* can also be embellished by personalizing rhythms or dynamics, and chord labels are provided for pianists who are comfortable playing their own chord voicings. In some cases, optional, written-out improvisations are provided. These can be performed "as is," embellished, or skipped, depending on the performers' preference.

The included audio features piano recordings that can be used as a rehearsal aid or to accompany a performance. Tempi were selected to fit the character of each accompaniment, and the optional piano solos were omitted to provide a more seamless singing experience for vocalists who utilize them as backing tracks.

I hope you find many hours of enjoyment exploring the *Singer's Jazz Anthology* series!

Brent Edstrom

ALL THE THINGS YOU ARE
from VERY WARM FOR MAY

Lyrics by OSCAR HAMMERSTEIN II
Music by JEROME KERN

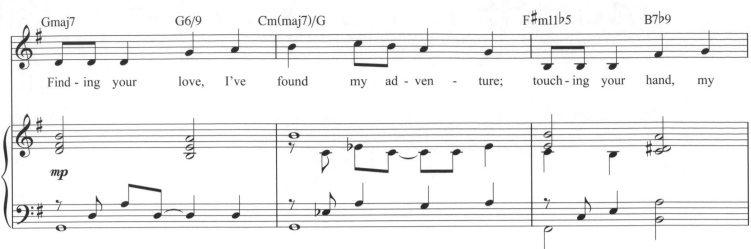

Find- ing your love, I've found my ad- ven - ture; touch-ing your hand, my

heart beats the fast - er. All that I want in all of this world is

you.

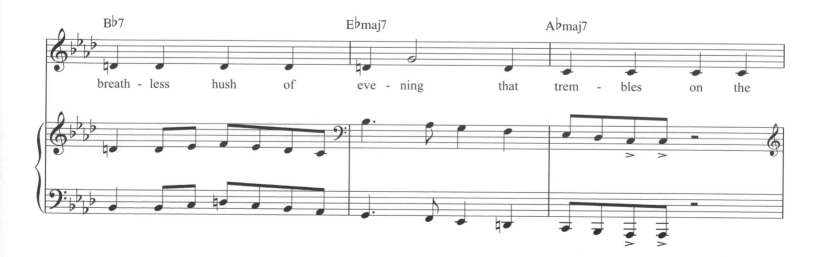

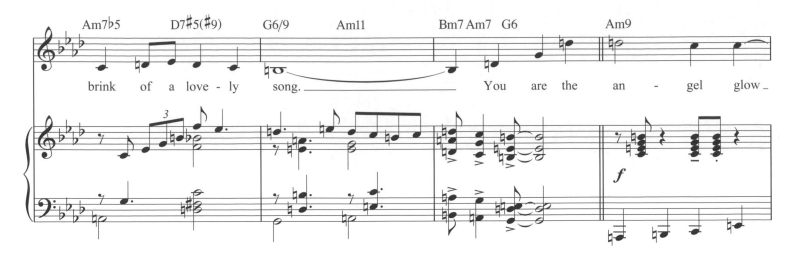

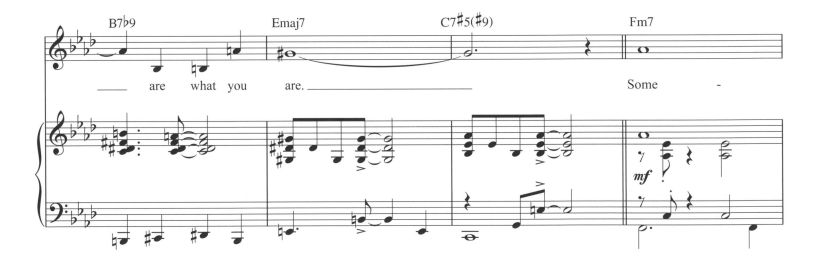

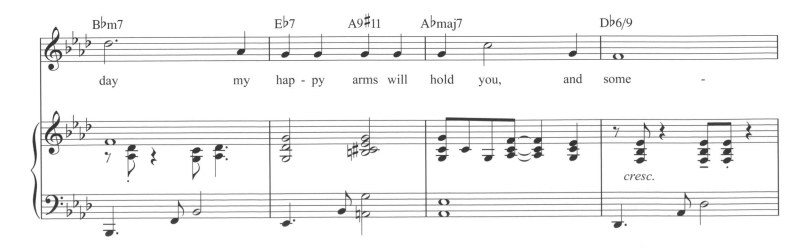

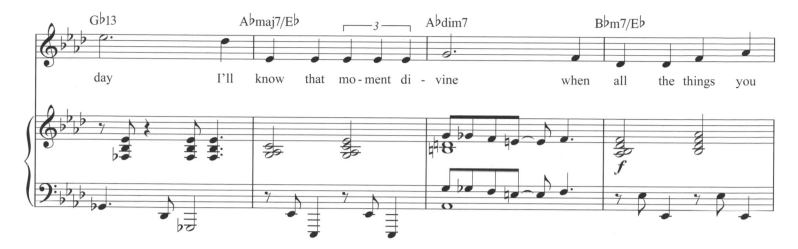

day   I'll   know   that mo - ment di - vine   when   all   the things   you

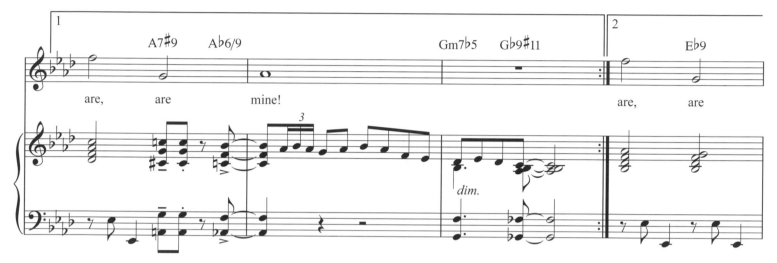

are,   are   mine!   are,   are

mine,   are mine, ___   are mine, ___   are mine, ___

all   the   things you   are,   arc   mine! _____

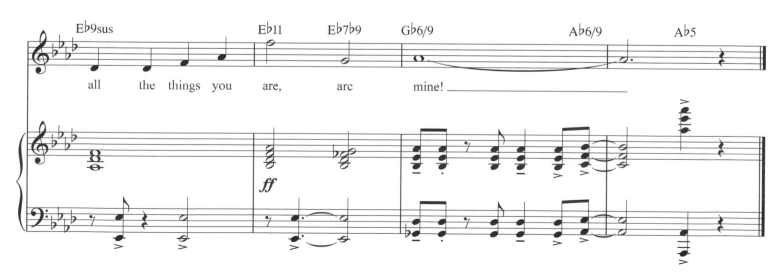

AUTUMN LEAVES

English lyric by JOHNNY MERCER
French lyric by JACQUES PREVERT
Music by JOSEPH KOSMA

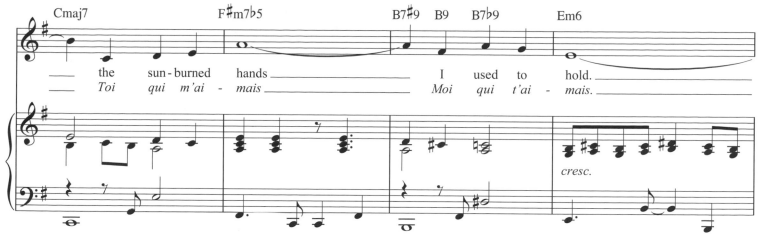

the sun-burned hands _____ I used to hold. _____
Toi qui m'ai - mais _____ Moi qui t'ai - mais. _____

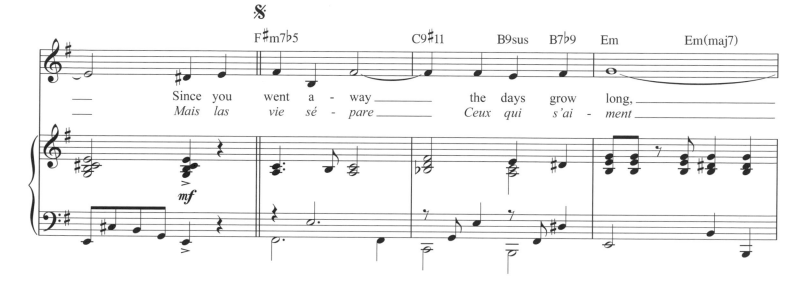

Since you went a - way _____ the days grow long, _____
Mais las vie sé - pare _____ Ceux qui s'ai - ment _____

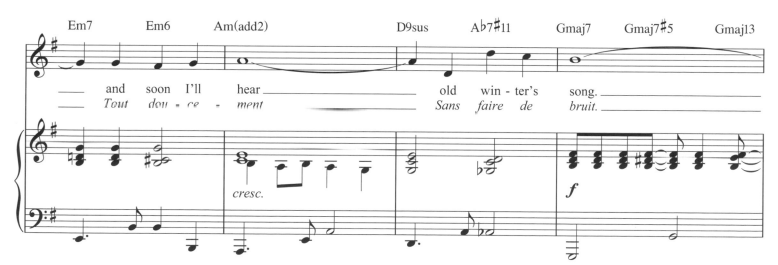

_____ and soon I'll hear _____ old win - ter's song. _____
_____ *Tout dou - ce - ment _____ Sans faire de bruit.* _____

But I miss you most of all, my dar - ling, _____
Et la mer ef - fa - ce sur le sa - ble _____

To Coda ⊕

G13　　　C9♯11　　　F♯m7♭5　　　B7♯5(♯9)

when au - tumn leaves start to
Les pas des a - ments dé - su -

To Chorus　　　　　　　　　　**D.S. al Coda** | **To Opt. Piano Solo**

Em6　　　　　　　　N.C.　　　　　　Em6

fall.　　　　　　　　Since you fall.
nis.　　　　　　　　*Mais las nis.*

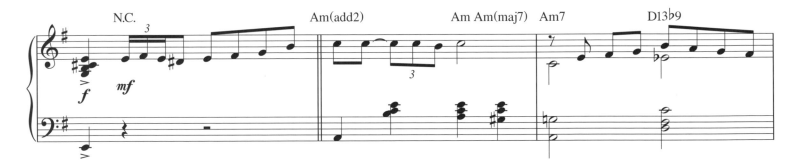

cresc.　　　　　　　f　　　　　　cresc.

N.C.　　　　　　Am(add2)　　　Am Am(maj7) Am7　　　D13♭9

f　mf

Gmaj9　Gmaj9♯5　Gmaj13　Cmaj7　　　　　　F♯m7♭5　　C13

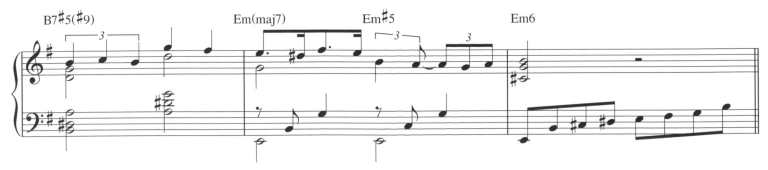

B7♯5(♯9)　　　　Em(maj7)　　　Em♯5　　　　Em6

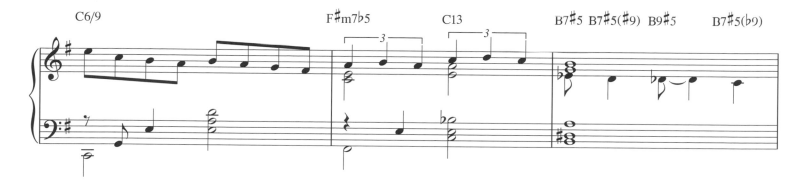

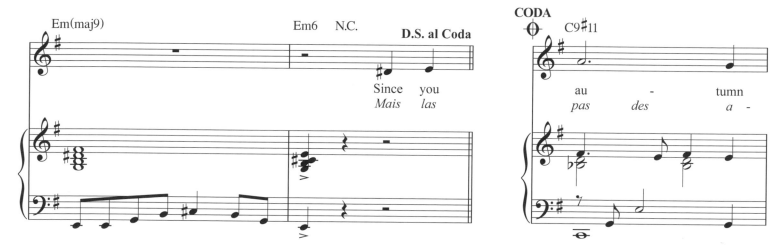

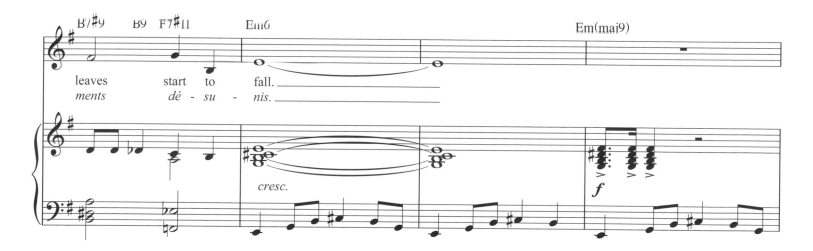

ALMOST LIKE BEING IN LOVE
from BRIGADOON

Lyrics by ALAN JAY LERNER
Music by FREDERICK LOEWE

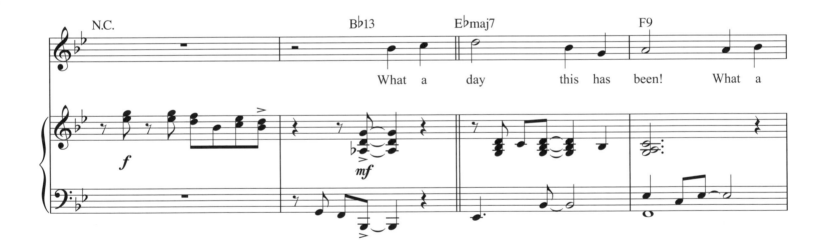

be - ing in love. _____ There's a

smile on my face for the whole hu - man

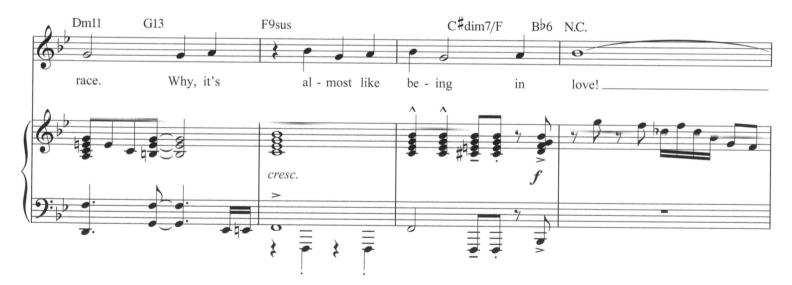

race. Why, it's al - most like be - ing in love! _____

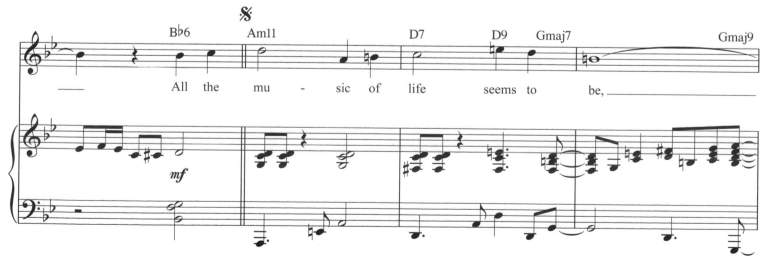

All the mu - sic of life seems to be, _____

like a bell that is ring-ing for me.

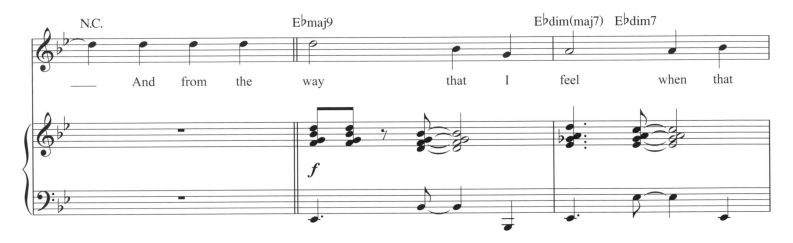

And from the way that I feel when that

bell starts to peal I would swear I was fall-ing, I could

To Coda

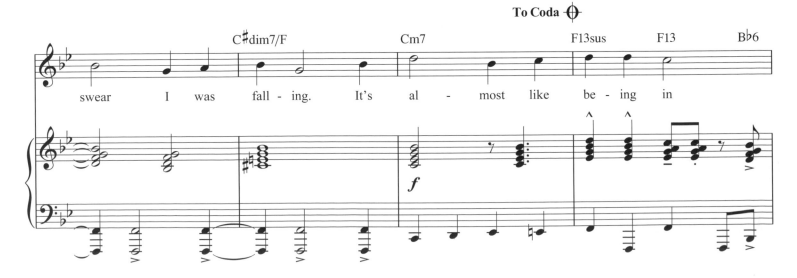

swear I was fall-ing. It's al-most like be-ing in

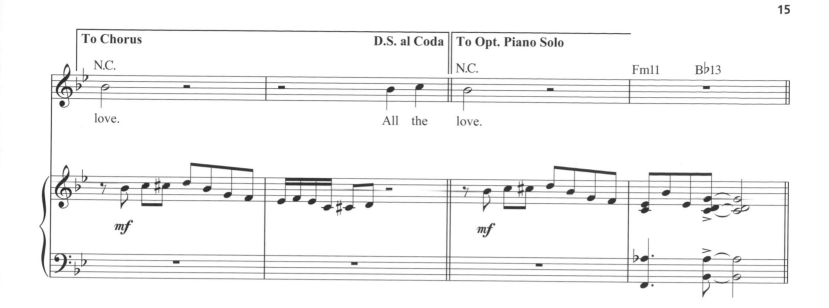

16

All the

be - ing in love.

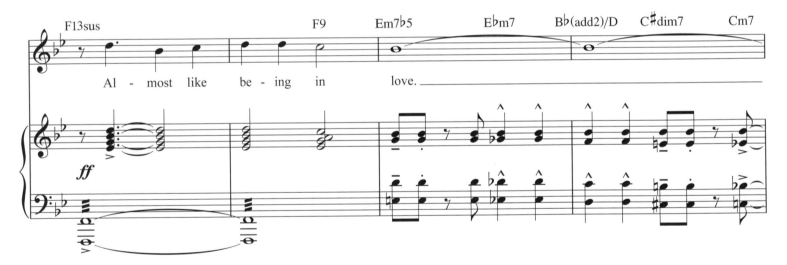

Al - most like be - ing in love.

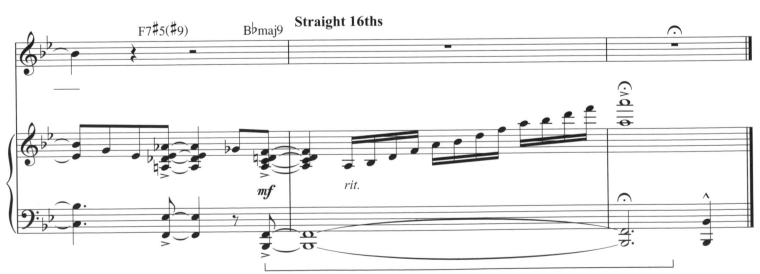

Straight 16ths

CHEEK TO CHEEK
from the RKO Radio Motion Picture TOP HAT

Words and Music by
IRVING BERLIN

Moderately fast Swing

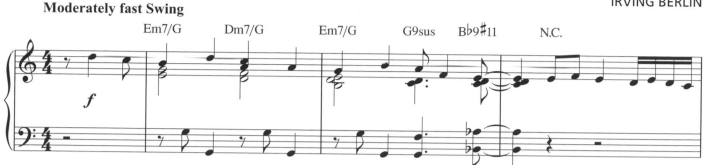

love to climb a moun - tain, and to reach the high - est peak, __
love to go out fish - ing in a riv - er or a creek, __

but it does - n't thrill me half as much __ as
but I don't en - joy it

danc - ing cheek to cheek. __ Oh, I half as much __ as

danc - ing cheek to cheek. __ Dance with me, __ I want my

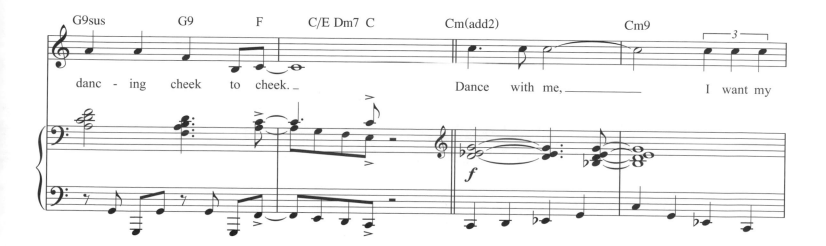

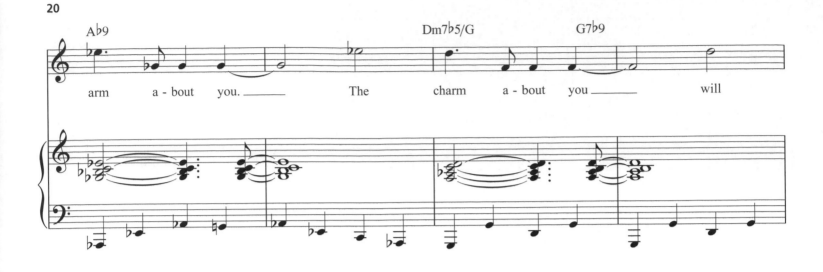

arm a - bout you. _____ The charm a - bout you _____ will

car - ry me through ___ to Heav - en, _____ I'm in

Heav - en. _____ And my heart beats so that I can hard - ly

speak. _____ And I seem to find the hap - pi - ness I

BLUE SKIES
from BETSY

Words and Music by
IRVING BERLIN

Moderate Swing

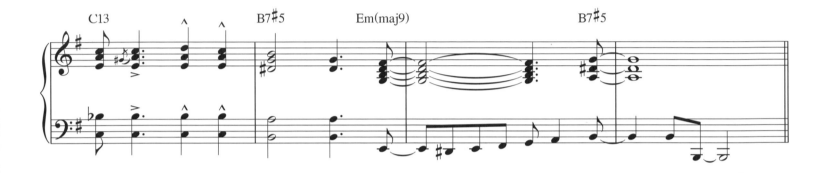

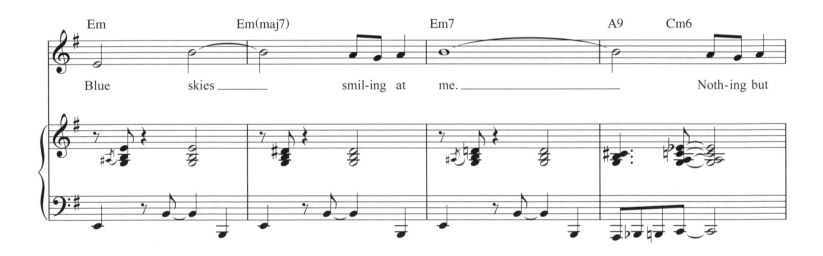

Blue skies _____ smil-ing at me. _____ Noth-ing but

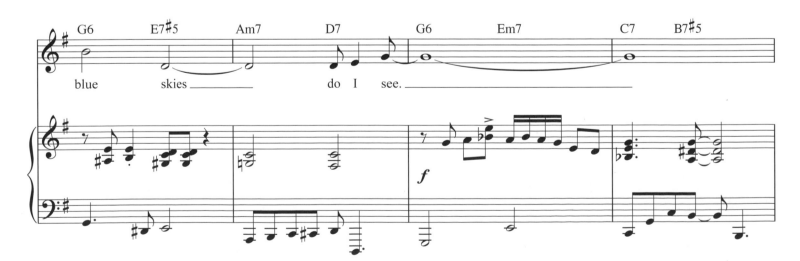

blue skies _____ do I see. _____

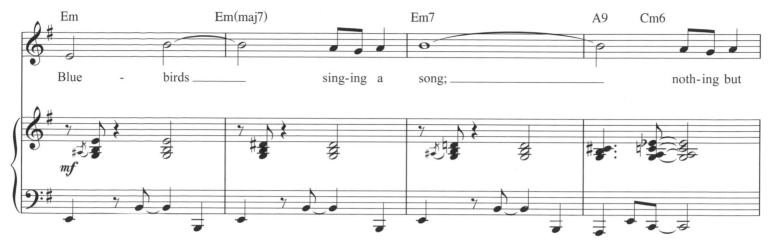

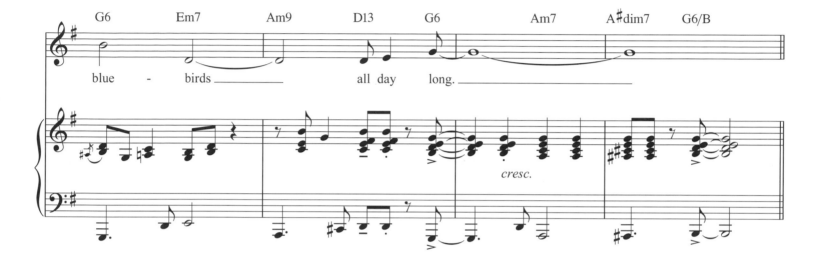

Blue days, _____ all of them gone. Noth-ing but

blue skies _____ from now on. _____

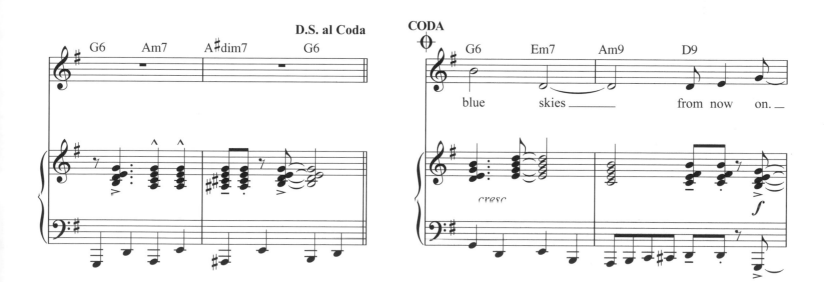

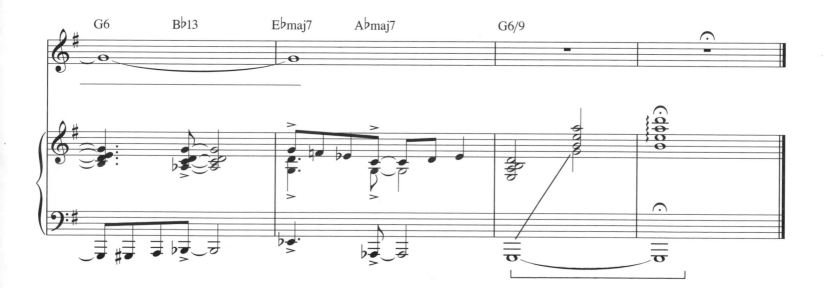

BODY AND SOUL
from THREE'S A CROWD

Words by EDWARD HEYMAN,
ROBERT SOUR and FRANK EYTON
Music by JOHN GREEN

me you're wrong-ing, I tell you I mean it,

I'm all for you, bod-y and soul! I can't be-lieve it, it's

hard to con-ceive it, that you'd turn a-way ro-mance. _

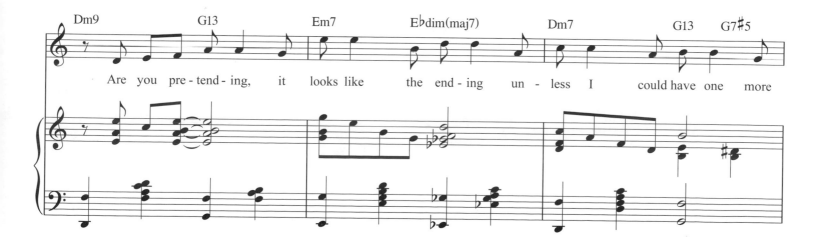

Are you pre-tend-ing, it looks like the end-ing un-less I could have one more

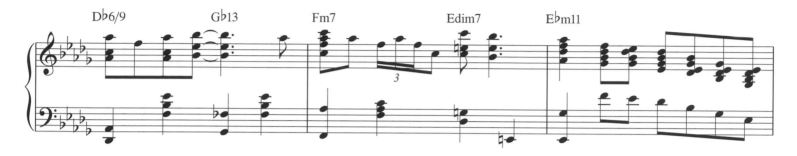

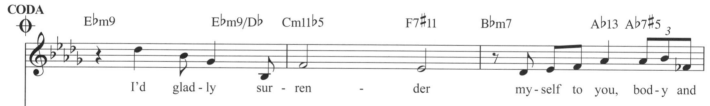

COME RAIN OR COME SHINE

from ST. LOUIS WOMAN

Words by JOHNNY MERCER
Music by HAROLD ARLEN

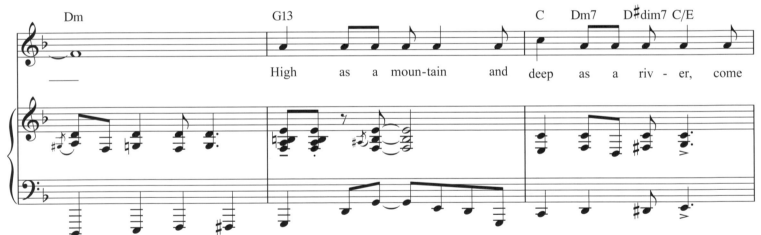

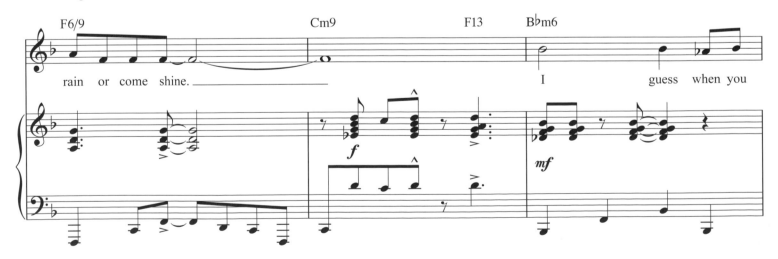

met me it was just one of those things,

but don't ev - er bet me 'cause I'm gon-na be true if you let me.

You're gon - na love me like no - bod-y's loved me, come rain or come shine.

Hap - py to-geth-er, un - hap - py to-geth-er, and

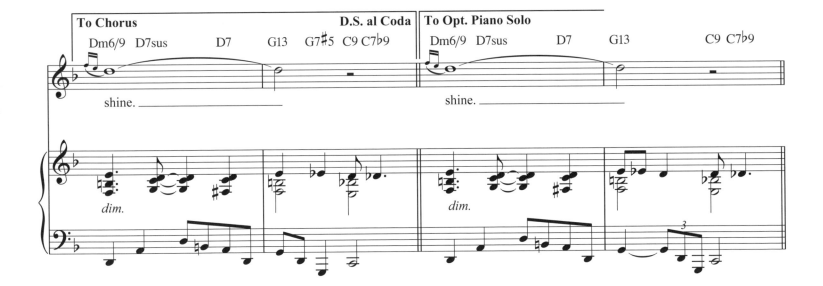

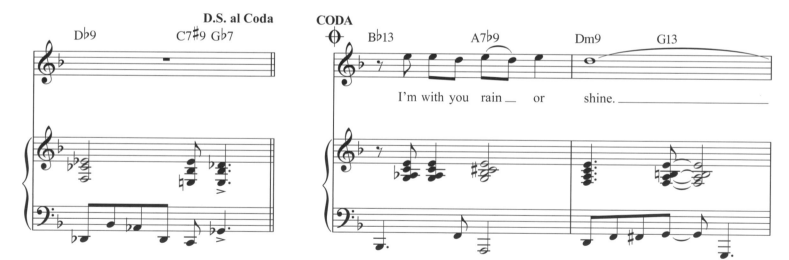

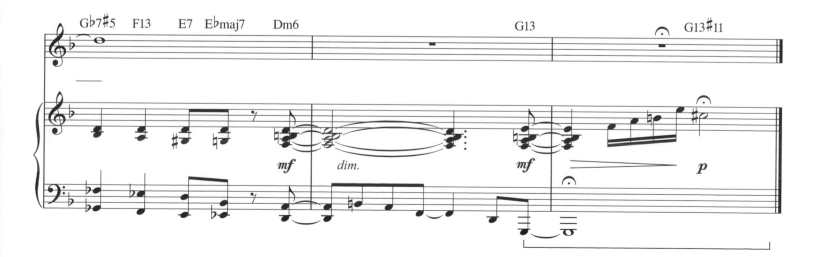

DO NOTHIN' TILL YOU HEAR FROM ME

Words and Music by DUKE ELLINGTON
and BOB RUSSELL

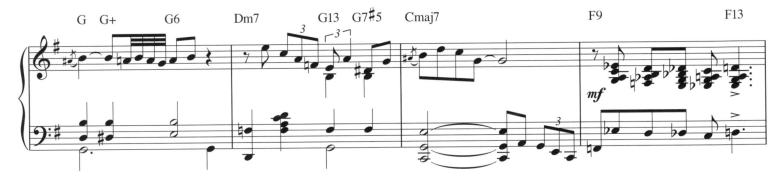

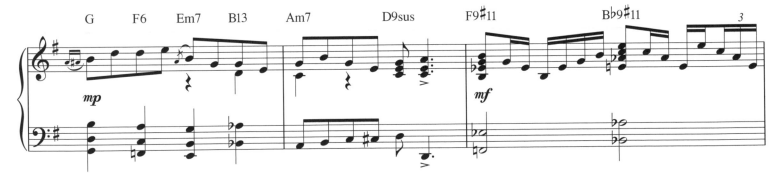

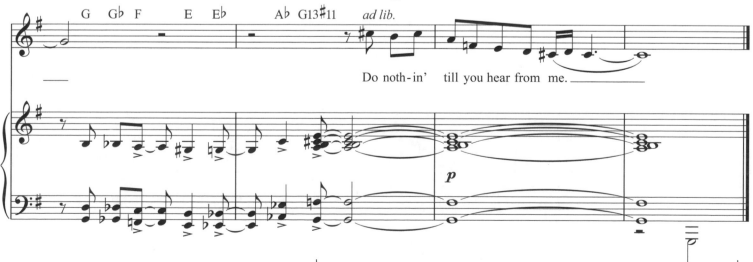

FLY ME TO THE MOON
(In Other Words)
featured in the Motion Picture ONCE AROUND

Words and Music by
BART HOWARD

Fly me to the moon, ___ and let me play a-mong the stars; ___ Let me see what spring ___ is like on

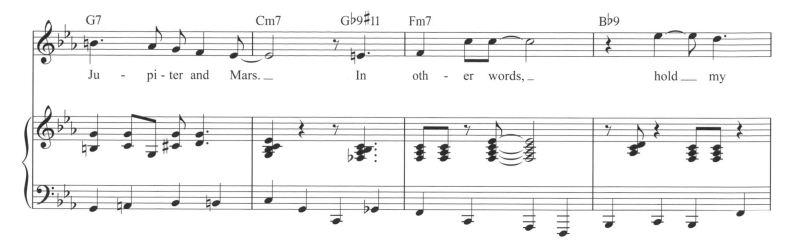

Ju - pi-ter and Mars. _ In oth - er words, _ hold __ my

hand! _____ In oth - er words, _ dar - ling,

kiss me! _____ Fill my heart with song, __ and let me

sing for-ev-er - more; __ you are all I long __ for, all I

To Coda

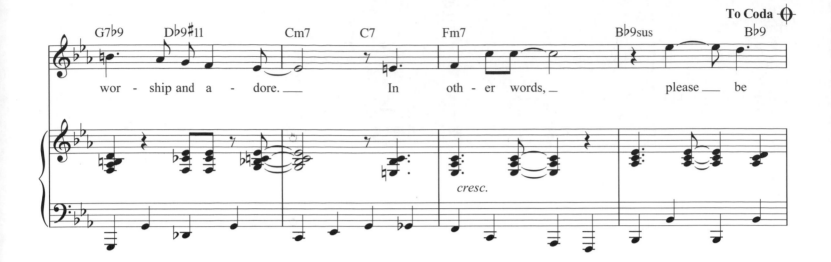

wor - ship and a - dore.___ In oth - er words,___ please___ be

true! _____ In oth - er words, _ I ___ love

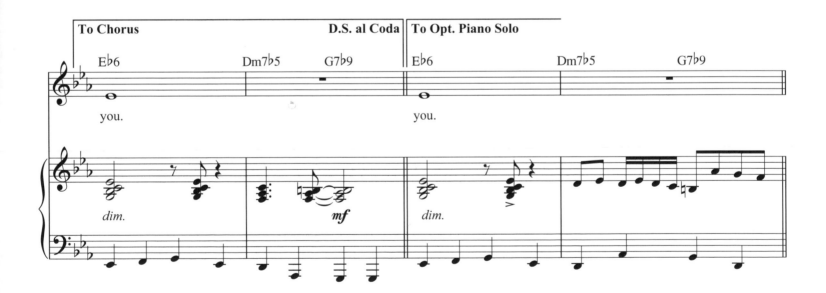

you.

you.

D.S. al Coda

true! _____ In oth - er words, _ I _____ love

you! _____

GEORGIA ON MY MIND

Words by STUART GORRELL
Music by HOAGY CARMICHAEL

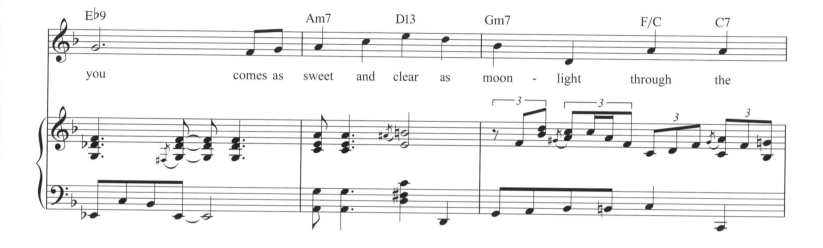

Still in peace - ful dreams I see ___ the road leads back to

you. ___ Geor - gia, ___ Geor - gia, ___

To Coda

no peace I find. Just an old sweet song keeps

To Chorus　　　　　　　　　　　　　　**D.S. al Coda**

Geor - gia on my mind. ___

To Opt. Piano Solo

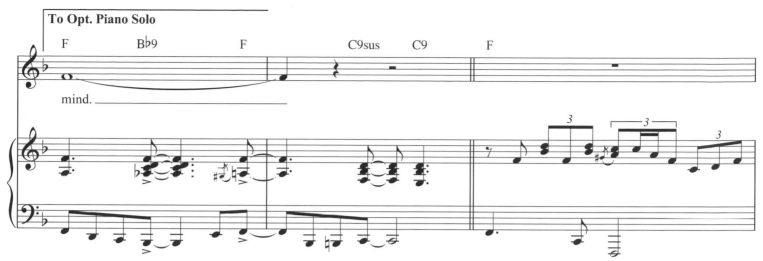

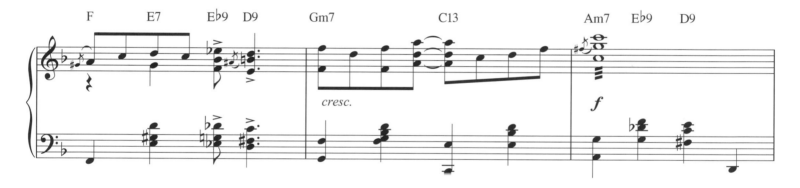

Double-time feel, Swing 16ths

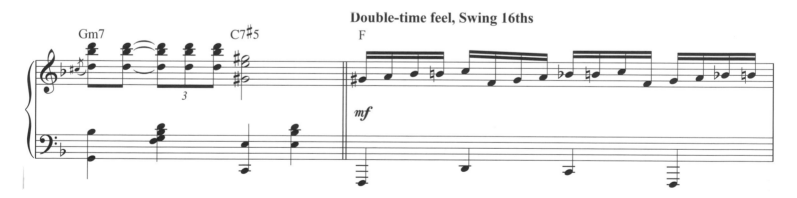

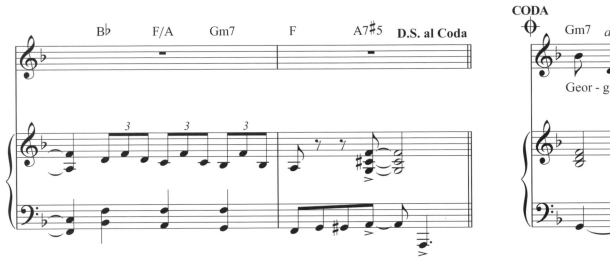

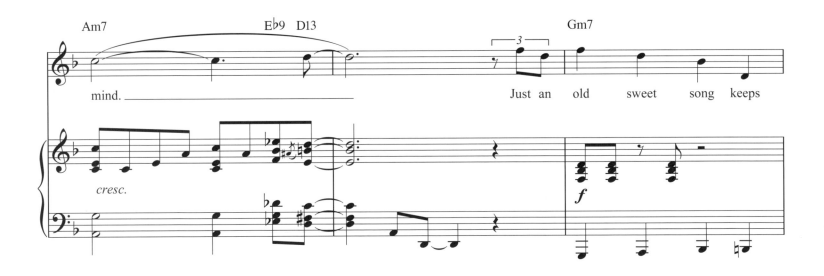

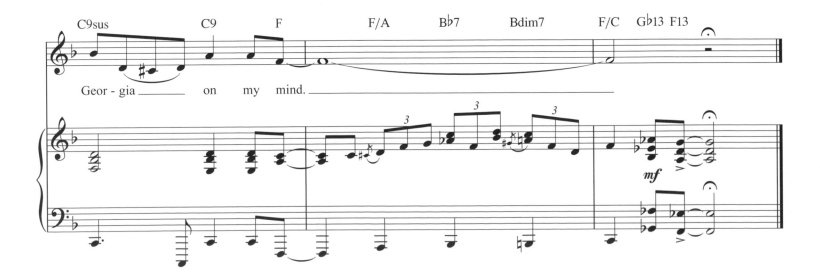

I CAN'T GET STARTED

from ZIEGFELD FOLLIES

Words by IRA GERSHWIN
Music by VERNON DUKE

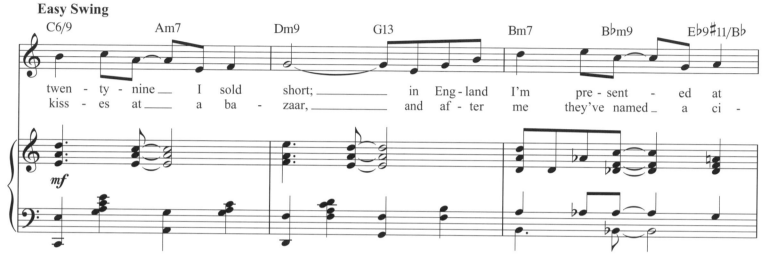

HONEYSUCKLE ROSE

from AIN'T MISBEHAVIN'
from TIN PAN ALLEY

Words by ANDY RAZAF
Music by THOMAS "FATS" WALLER

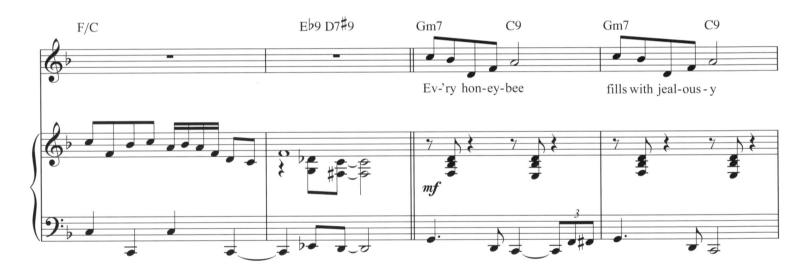

Ev-'ry hon-ey-bee fills with jeal-ous-y

when they see you out with me; I don't blame them, good - ness knows, _____ Hon-ey-suck-le

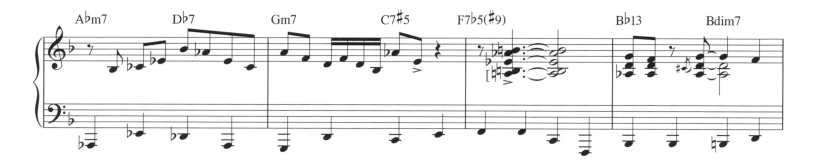

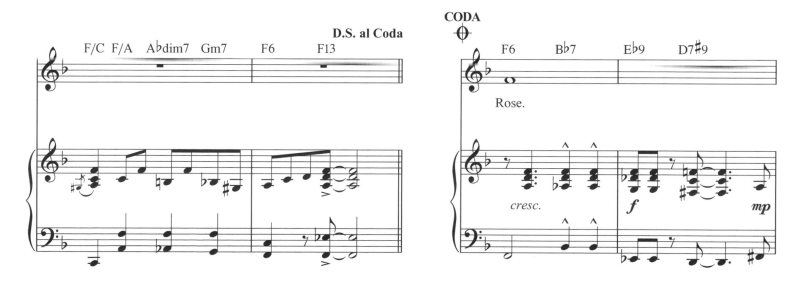

HOW HIGH THE MOON

from TWO FOR THE SHOW

Lyrics by NANCY HAMILTON
Music by MORGAN LEWIS

Bright Swing

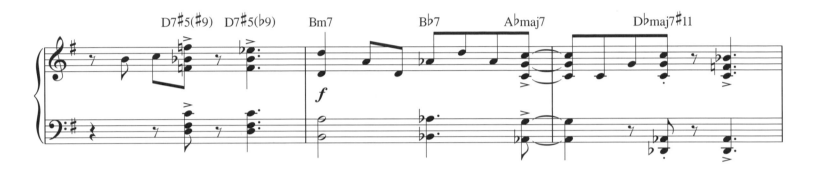

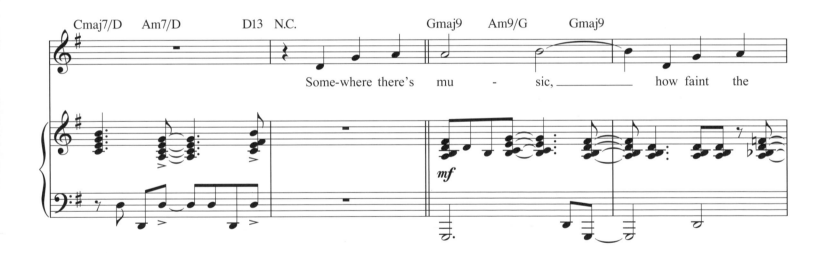

Some-where there's mu - sic, _____ how faint the

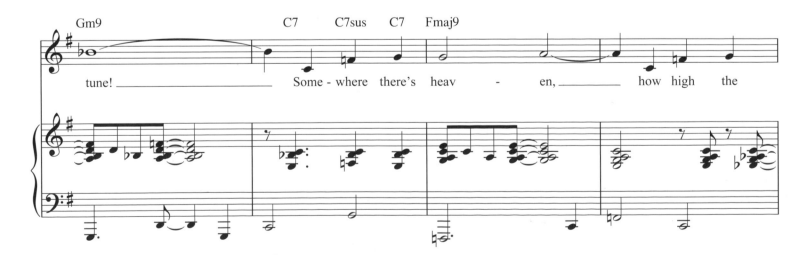

tune! _____ Some - where there's heav - en, _____ how high the

Fm9   Bb13   Ebmaj7   Am7b5   D7b9

moon! _____ There is no moon a - bove when love is far __ a - way,

Gm   Am7b5   D7   Gmaj9   Am9   D13

too, _____ till __ it comes true _____ that you love

cresc.

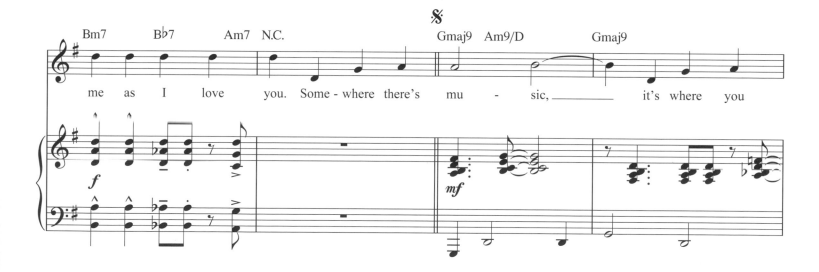

Bm7   Bb7   Am7 N.C.   Gmaj9 Am9/D   Gmaj9

me as I love you. Some - where there's mu - sic, _____ it's where you

f   *mf*

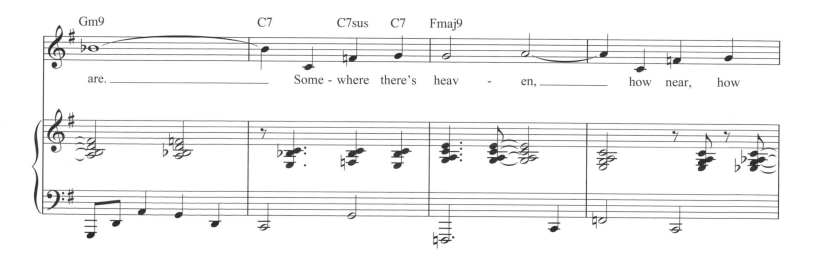

Gm9   C7   C7sus   C7 Fmaj9

are. _____ Some - where there's heav - en, _____ how near, how

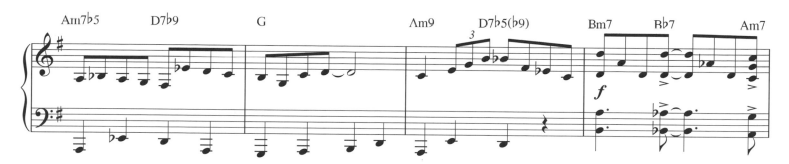

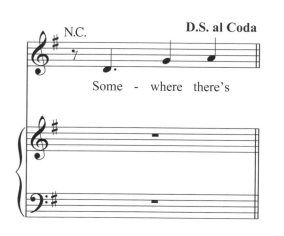

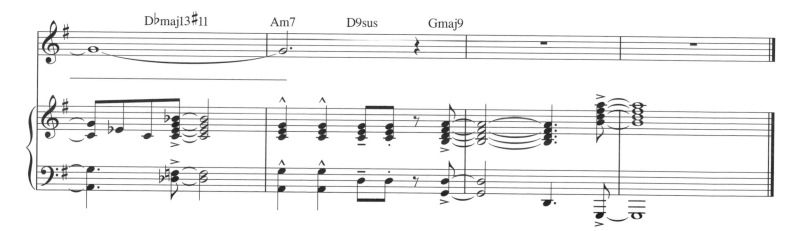

IT MIGHT AS WELL BE SPRING

from STATE FAIR

Lyrics by OSCAR HAMMERSTEIN II
Music by RICHARD RODGERS

IT'S ONLY A PAPER MOON

Lyric by BILLY ROSE and E.Y. "YIP" HARBURG
Music by HAROLD ARLEN

Up-beat Swing

Say, it's on-ly a pa-per moon, _ sail - ing o - ver a

card - board sea, _ but it would-n't be make be - lieve, _ if you _

_ be - lieved _ in me. _ Yes, it's on - ly a can - vas sky, _

hang - ing o - ver a mus - lin tree, _ but it would-n't be make be - lieve, _ if you _

_ be - lieved _ in me. _ With - out your love, it's a

hon - ky-tonk pa - rade. With - out your love, it's a

mel - o - dy played in a pen - ny ar - cade. It's a Bar-num and Bai - ley world, _

just as pho-ny as it can be, ___ But it would-n't be make be-lieve, ___ if you ___

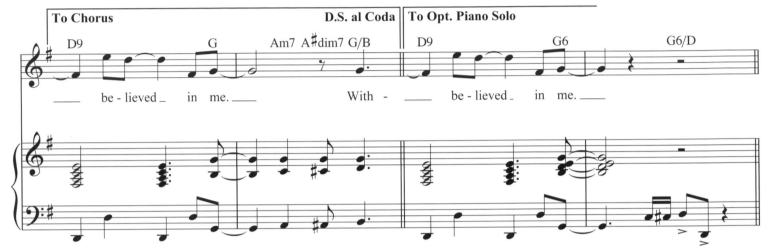

___ be-lieved ___ in me. ___ With - ___ be-lieved ___ in me. ___

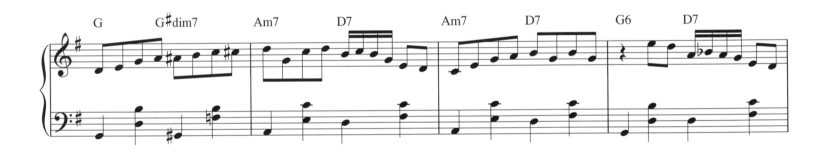

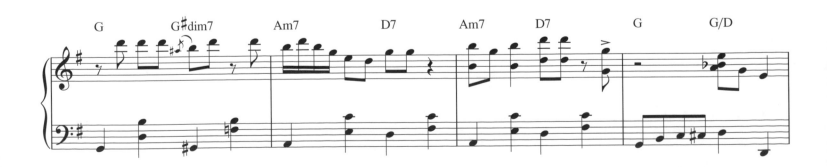

MISTY

Words by JOHNNY BURKE
Music by ERROLL GARNER

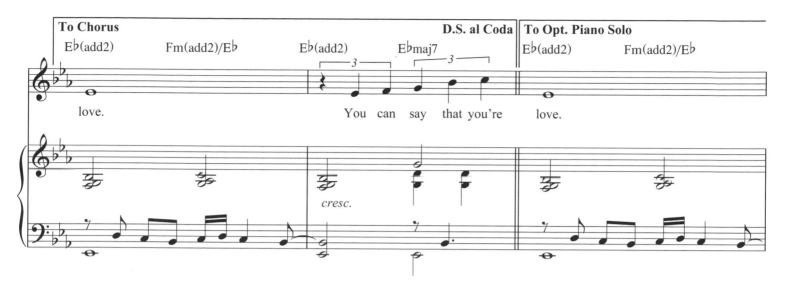

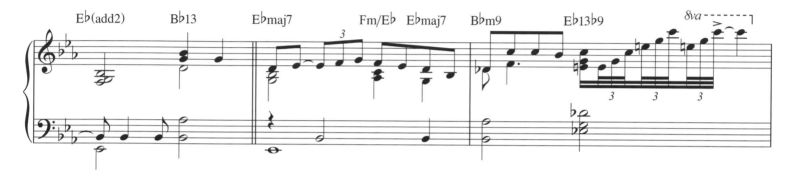

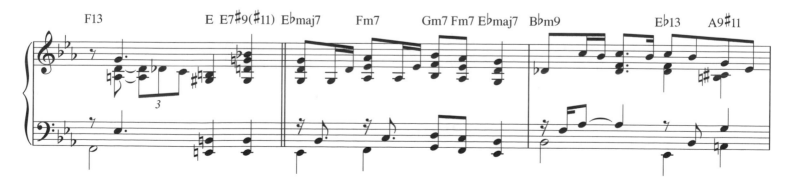

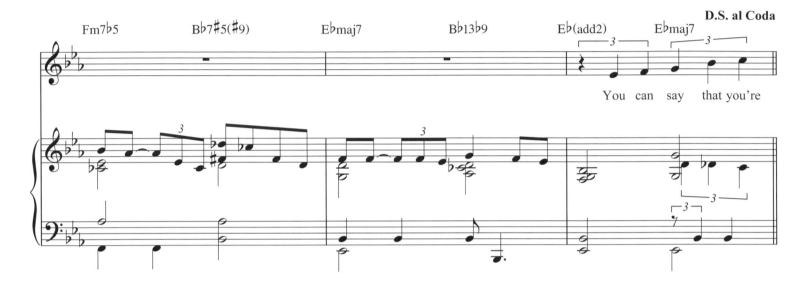

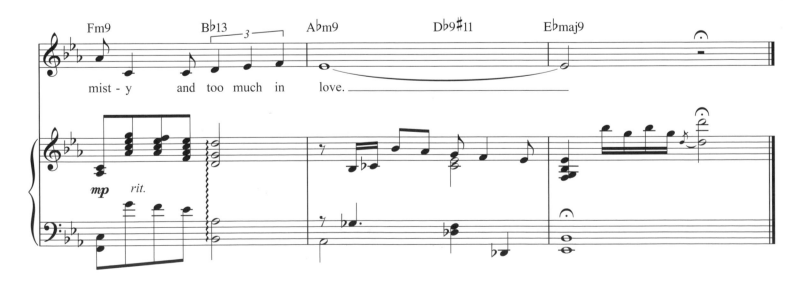

ROUTE 66

By BOBBY TROUP

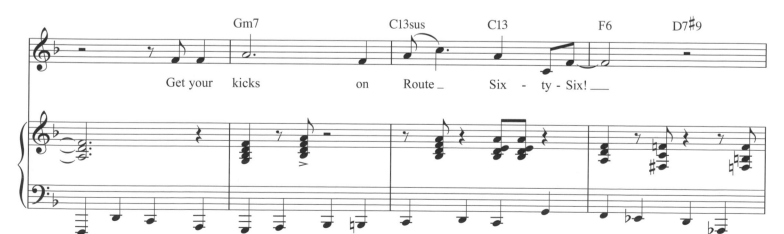

It winds _____ from Chi - ca - go to L. A., _____

more than two _____ thou-sand miles all the way. _____

Get your kicks on Route _ Six - ty - Six! _____

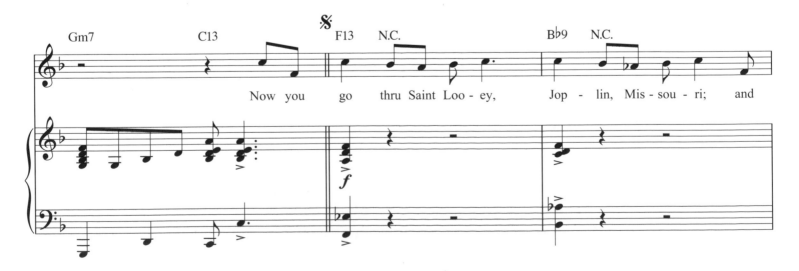

Now you go thru Saint Loo - ey, Jop - lin, Mis - sou - ri; and

O - kla - ho - ma Cit - y is might - y pret - ty. You'll see ___ Am - a -

ril - lo, ___ Gal - lup, New Mex - i - co, ___

Flag - staff, Ar - i - zo - na; don't for - get Wi - no - na, King - man, Bar - stow,

San Ber - nar - di - no. Won't you ___ get hip to this time - ly tip: ___

When you ___ make that Cal - i - for - nia trip, ___

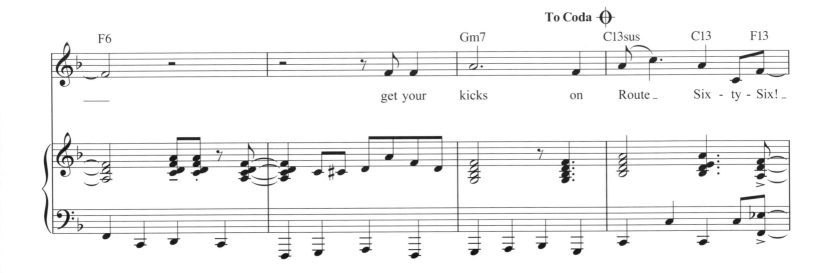

To Coda

get your kicks on Route ___ Six - ty - Six!

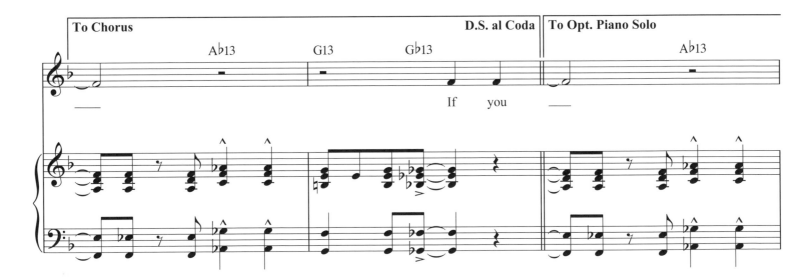

To Chorus

D.S. al Coda | **To Opt. Piano Solo**

If you ___

75

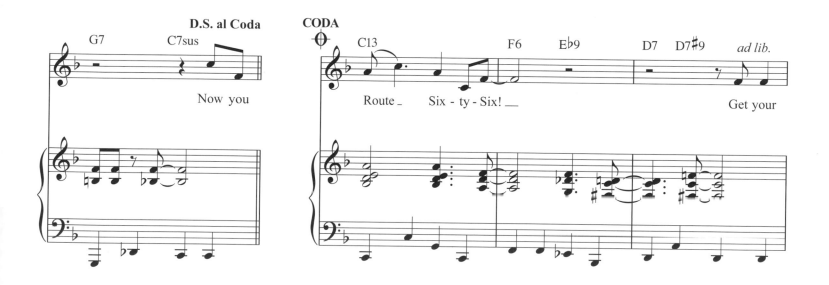

MY ROMANCE
from JUMBO

Words by LORENZ HART
Music by RICHARD RODGERS

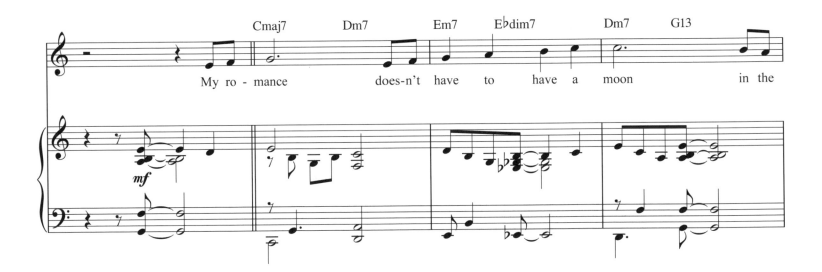

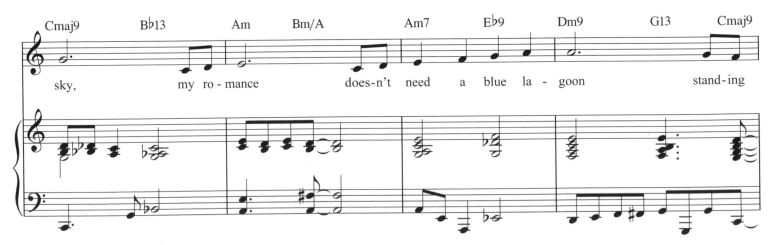

by; no month of May, no twin - kling

stars, no hide - a - way, no soft gui -

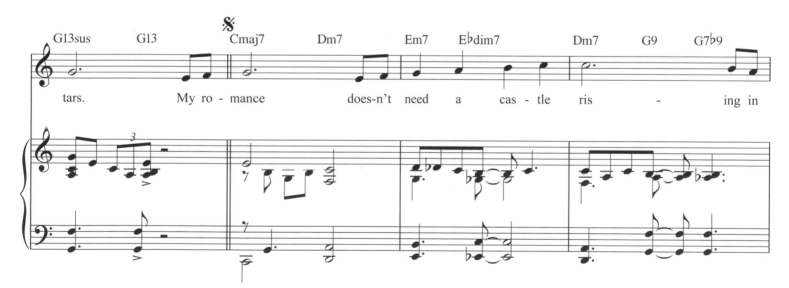

tars. My ro - mance does-n't need a cas - tle ris - ing in

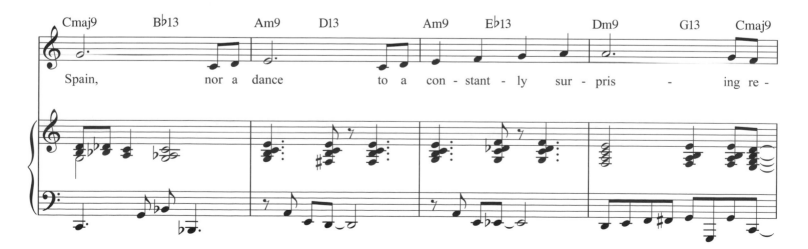

Spain, nor a dance to a con - stant - ly sur - pris - ing re -

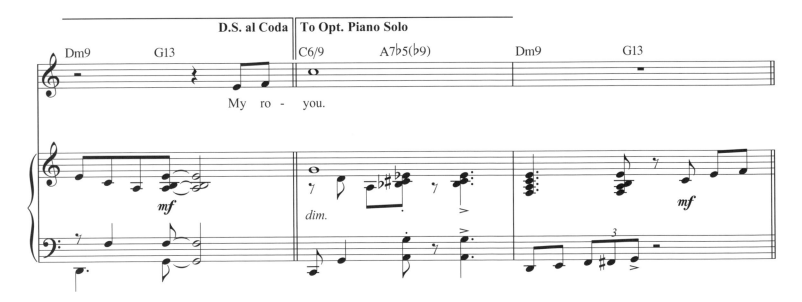

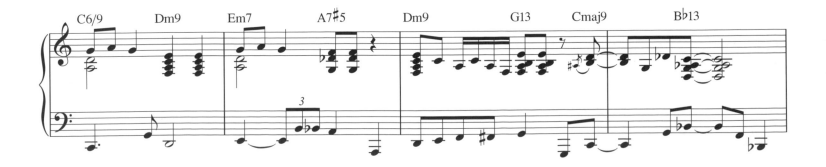

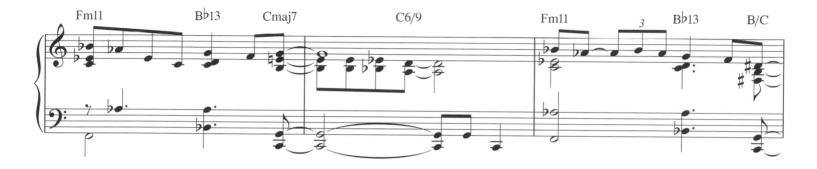

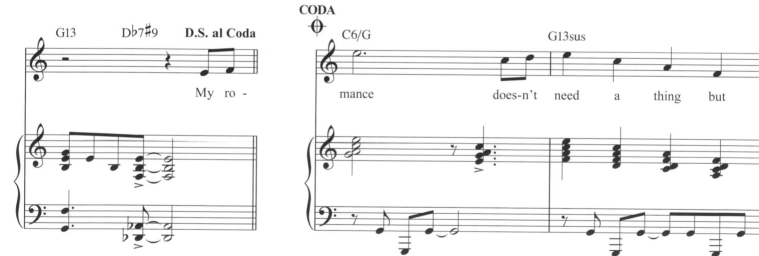

My ro -

mance does-n't need a thing but

you.

THE NEARNESS OF YOU
from the Paramount Picture ROMANCE IN THE DARK

Words by NED WASHINGTON
Music by HOAGY CARMICHAEL

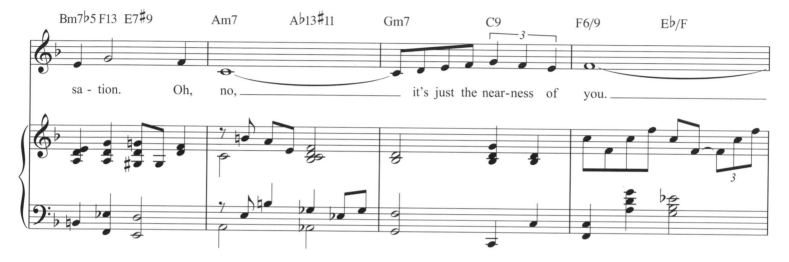

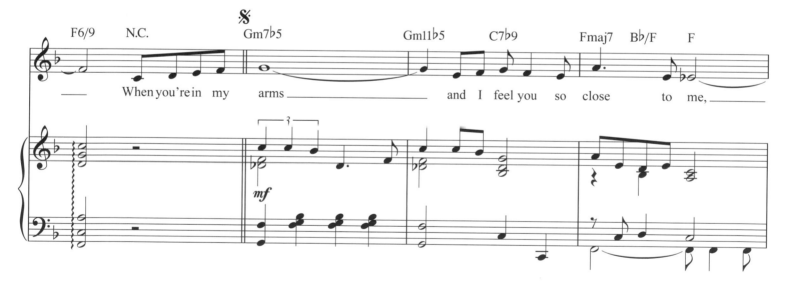

I need no soft lights to en-chant me if

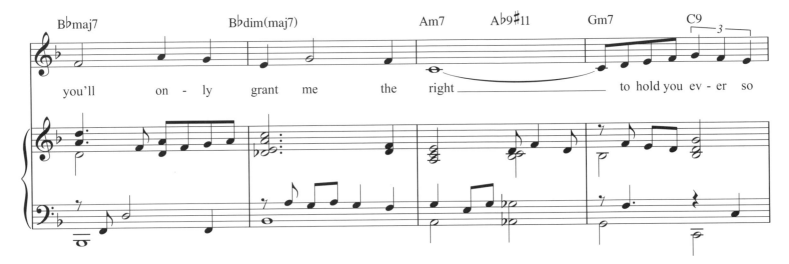

you'll on-ly grant me the right _____ to hold you ev-er so

To Coda ✛

tight, _____ and to feel in the night the near-ness of

To Chorus   **D.S. al Coda** | **To Opt. Piano Solo**

you. _____   When you're in my   you.

SOME OTHER TIME
from ON THE TOWN

Lyrics by BETTY COMDEN
and ADOLPH GREEN
Music by LEONARD BERNSTEIN

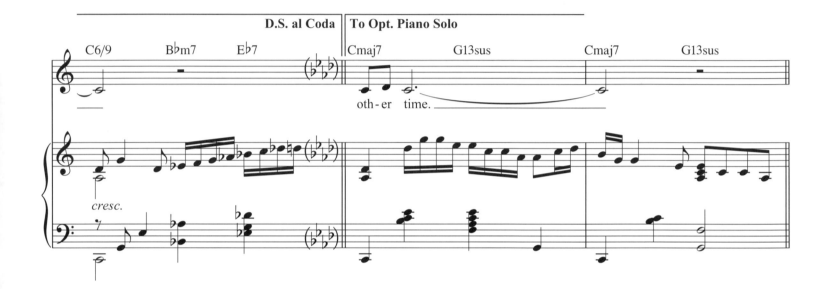

D.S. al Coda

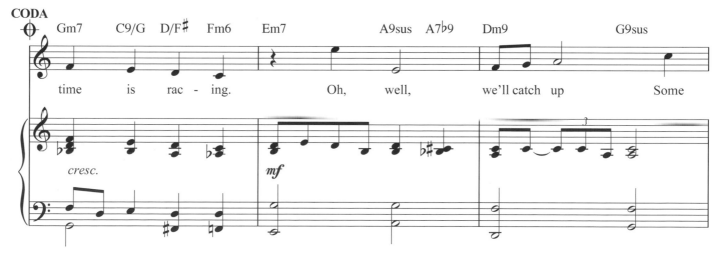

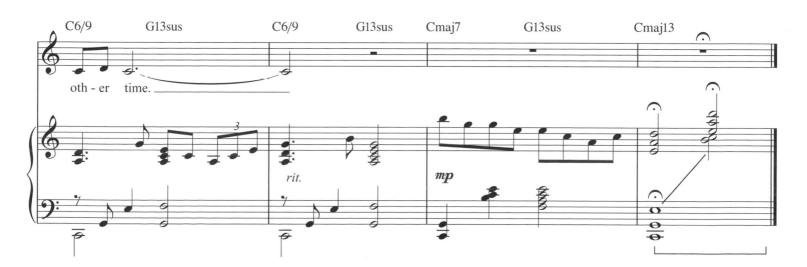

STARDUST

Words by MITCHELL PARISH
Music by HOAGY CARMICHAEL

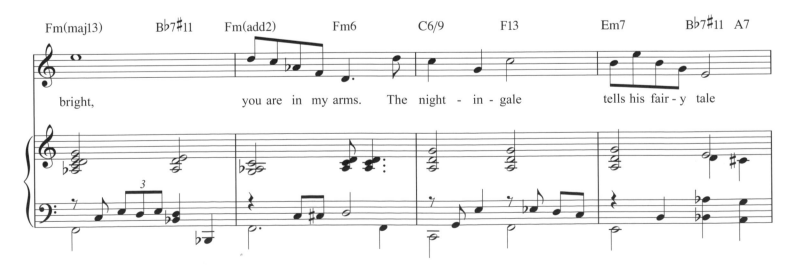

(There Is)
NO GREATER LOVE

Words by MARTY SYMES
Music by ISHAM JONES

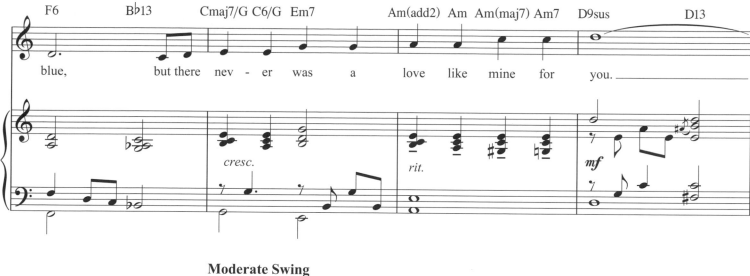

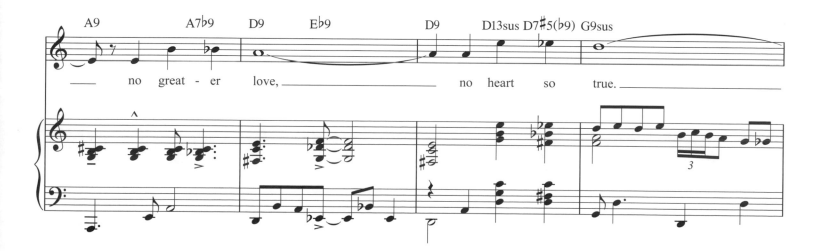

There is no great-er thrill than what you bring to me,

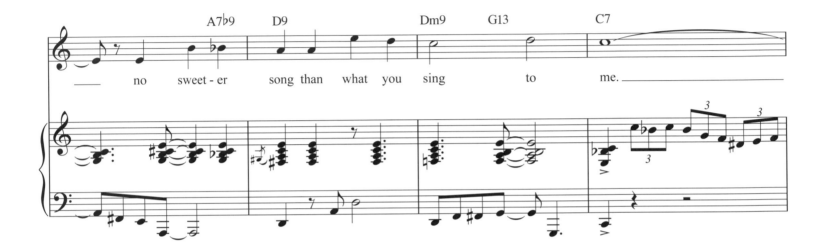

no sweet-er song than what you sing to me.

You're the sweet-est thing

I have ev-er known, and to think that you are mine a-

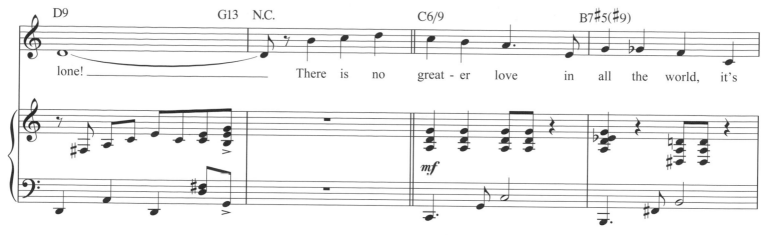

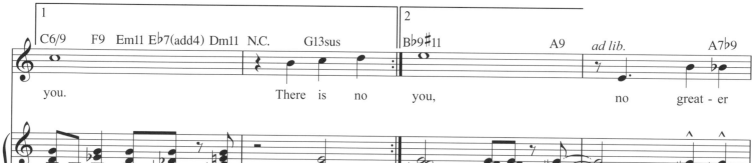

THE VERY THOUGHT OF YOU

Words and Music by
RAY NOBLE

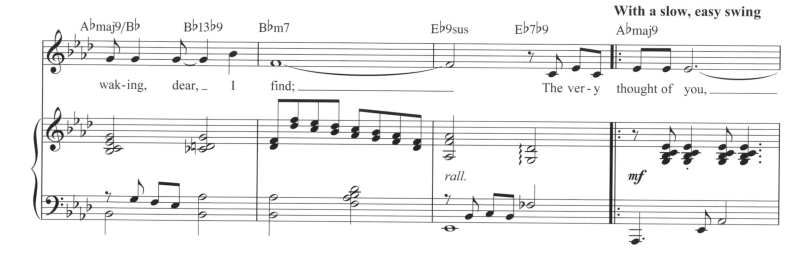

day - dream, I'm hap - py as a king, and fool - ish though it

may seem, to me _____ that's ev -'ry - thing. The mere i -

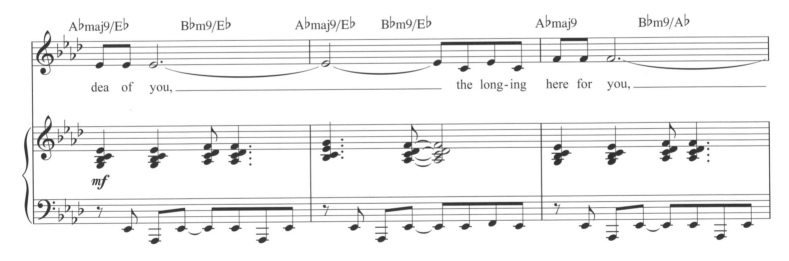

dea of you, _____ the long-ing here for you, _____

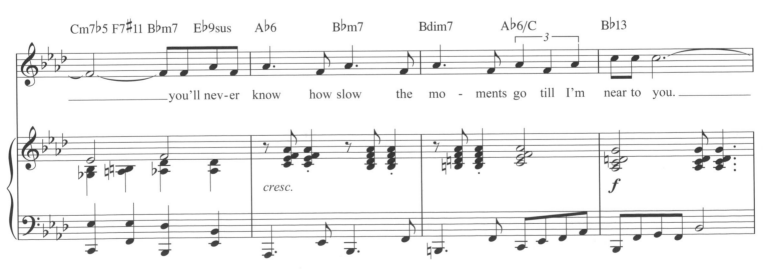

_____ you'll nev-er know how slow the mo - ments go till I'm near to you. _____

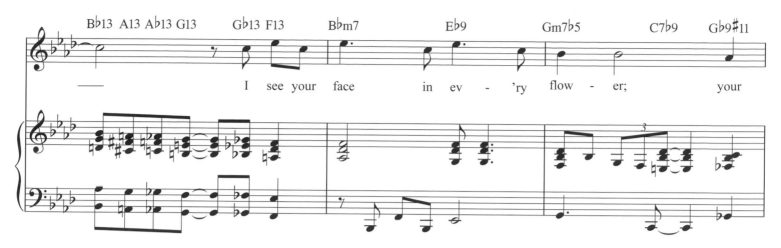

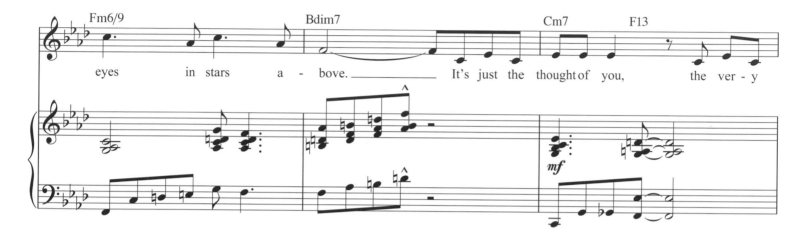

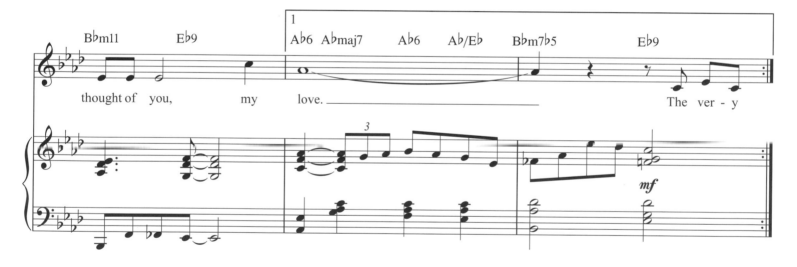

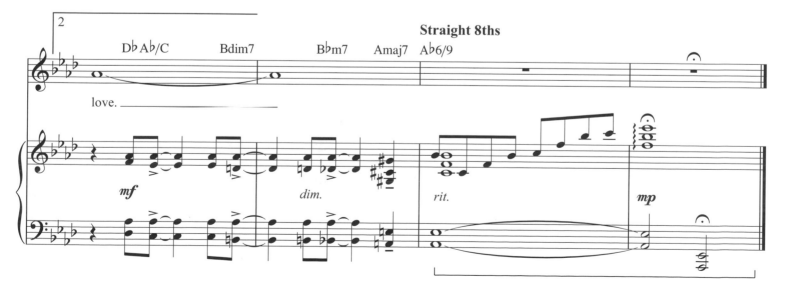

WHEN I FALL IN LOVE
from ONE MINUTE TO ZERO

Words by EDWARD HEYMAN
Music by VICTOR YOUNG

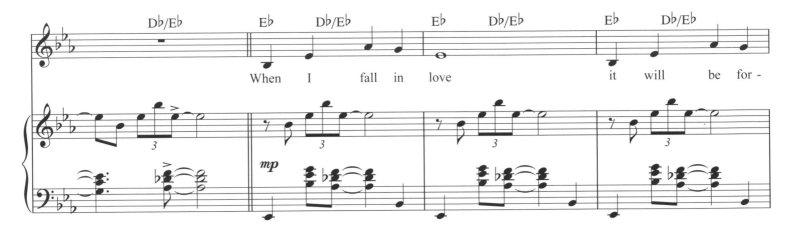

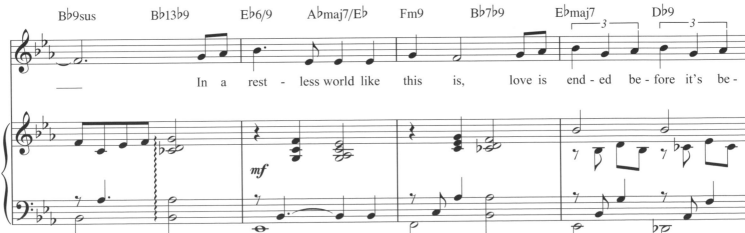

feel   that   way   too   is   when   I   fall   in   love   with

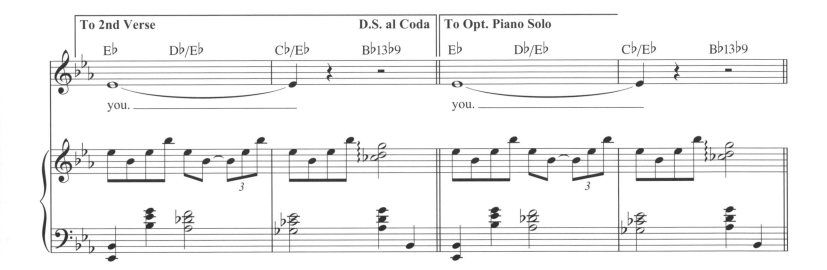

you. _____   you. _____

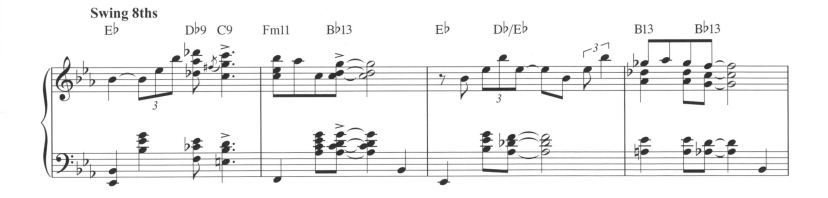

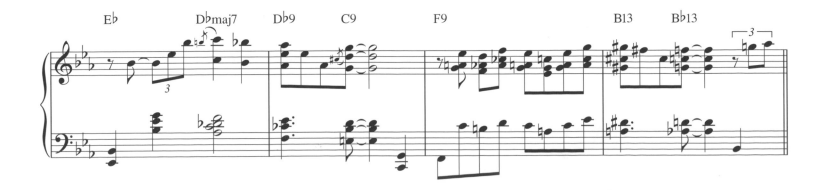

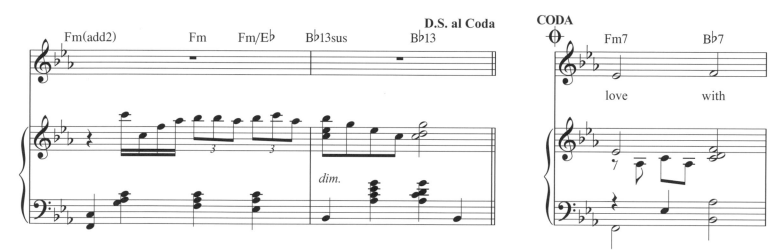

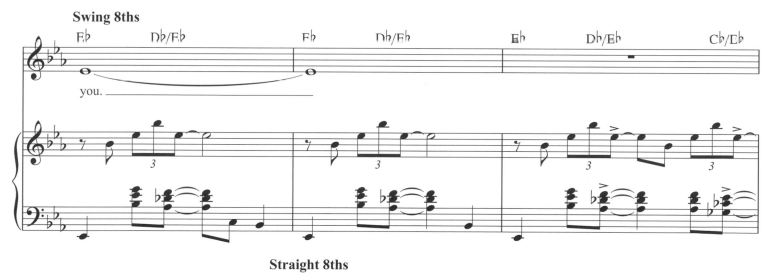

TENDERLY
from TORCH SONG

Lyric by JACK LAWRENCE
Music by WALTER GROSS

Moderate Swing

The eve-ning breeze ca-ressed the

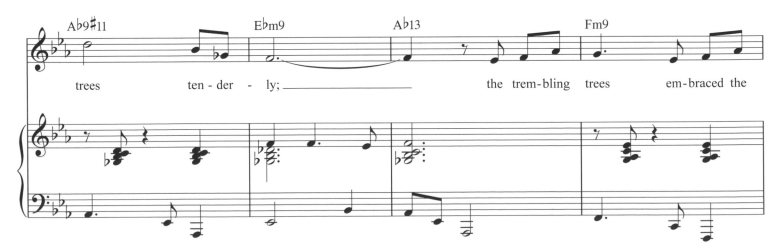

trees ten-der-ly; _____ the trem-bling trees em-braced the

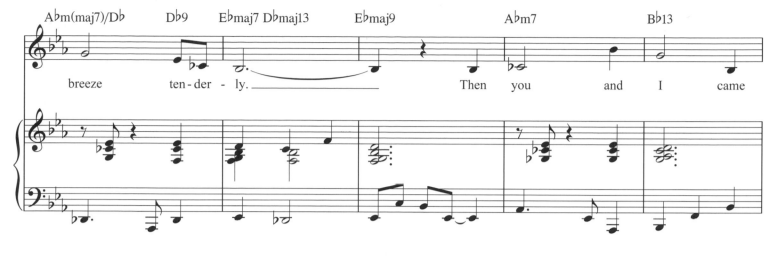

breeze ten-der-ly. _____ Then you and I came

wan-der-ing by and lost in a sigh were

we. _____ The shore was kissed by sea and mist ten-der-

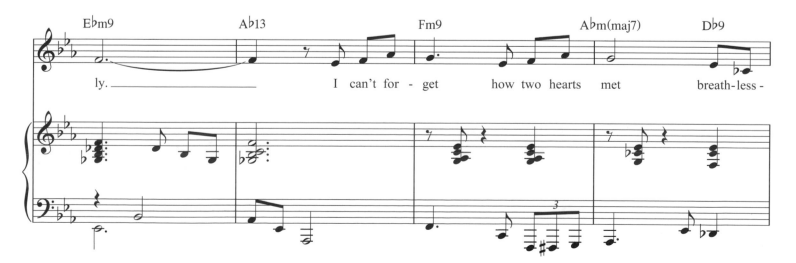

ly. _____ I can't for-get how two hearts met breath-less-

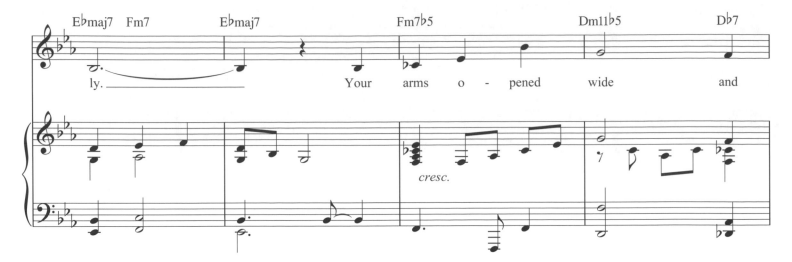

Your arms o - pened wide and

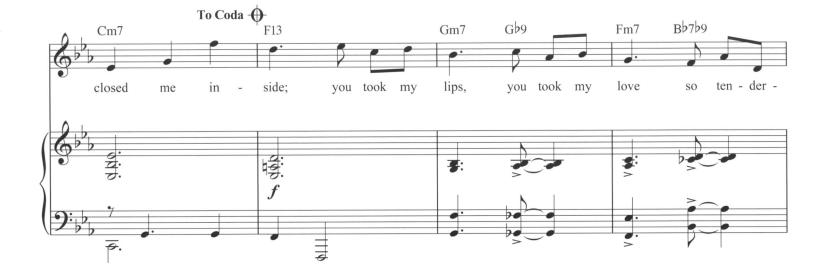

closed me in - side; you took my lips, you took my love so ten - der -

ly. The eve-ning ly.

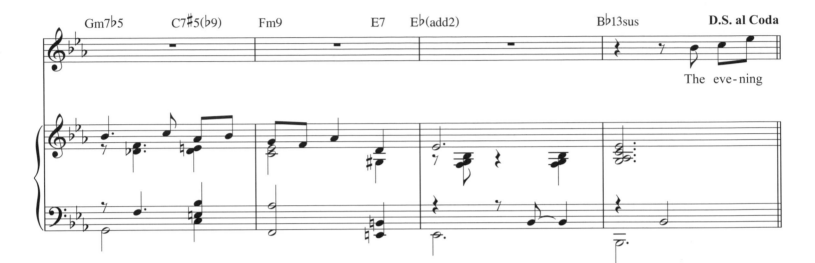

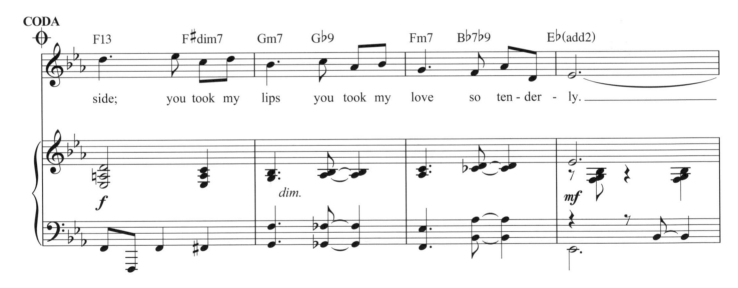

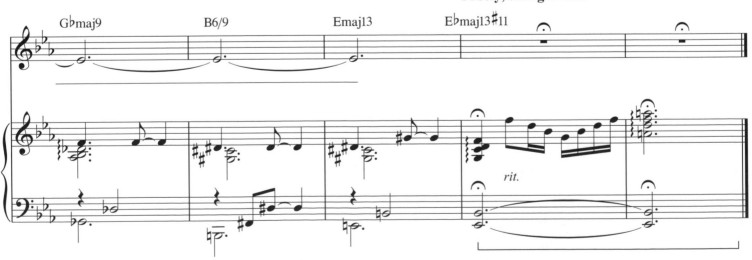